Spiritual Protection

Biblical Truth Simply Explained

Spiritual Protection

Lance Lambert

Chosen Books

A Division of Baker Book House Co
Grand Rapids, Michigan 49516

Published in the USA in 2004 by Chosen Books
a division of Baker Book House Company
P.O. Box 6287, Grand Rapids, MI 49516-6287
www.bakerbooks.com

Originally published under the title *Explaining Spiritual Protection* by
Sovereign World Limited of Tonbridge, Kent, England

Printed in the United States of America

Library of Congress Cataloging-in-Publication Data
Lambert, Lance.
    [Explaining spiritual protection]
    Spiritual protection / Lance Lambert.
        p. cm. — (Biblical truth simply explained)
    Originally published: Explaining spiritual protection. Tonbridge, Kent,
England: Sovereign World Ltd., 1991.
    ISBN 0-8007-9366-8 (pbk.)
    1. Spiritual warfare. I. Title. II. Series.

BV4509.5.L36 2004
235'.4—dc22

2003062502

Notes for Study Leaders

This book is a biblical and practical study of spiritual protection. The teaching is not just meant to be discussed—it is to be acted on, here and now. Five study questions at the end of each chapter are designed to help members of a study group both to think about and to engage personally with this subject.

As a leader, you will need to balance the needs of individuals with those of the entire group. Don't be surprised if different opinions and feelings arise during the study, particularly when answering certain questions. It is wise not to get side-tracked and devote too much time to any one person's thoughts but to enable everyone in the group to share and to respond to the positive message of the book.

Encourage group members to read one chapter prior to each meeting and consider each issue in advance. Reviewing the content of the chapter at the meeting will refresh everyone's memory and avoid embarrassing those who have not managed to do the "homework." It will also help members to share openly if the study takes place in a receptive, encouraging atmosphere.

Praying together and asking for God's help will help everyone to take hold of the truths presented. Our hope is that as readers work through the issue of spiritual protection they will become more secure in Christ and more fruitful in every area of their lives.

May God bless you as you study this material yourself and lead others in doing so.

Contents

Introduction

In these days, the Lord is calling the Church around the world to battle stations. More than ever before, we need to understand the enemy facing us. We also need to understand the rules of battle and how we can fight our enemy from a place of complete safety and protection.

I believe that one of the most essential things for Christians to know is how to be protected, or "covered," by Christ, and how to remain covered. Yet this vitally important subject is very often overlooked in the teachings of the Church, and the results are tragic: many casualties among believers, both young and old.

There is a war on against the Church at large. Satan's strategy is to lure Christians out of a place of safety into an exposed position. None of us is safe from his wiles unless we can recognize the danger and learn to counteract it.

The enemy's objective is to destroy our spiritual life, our home life and our role in the Church. We must wake up to his strategies: the ways in which he will try to sabotage our walk with God. Our Lord has the victory, but in our ignorance, many of us let the enemy continue to knock us down.

This little book will help us begin to grasp what is happening in the spirit realm and also show us what to do about it. As we better learn to understand Satan's plans, we can alert others in the battle. I am as much a student in these matters as anyone else. Let us learn together and so strengthen the Church of our Lord, Jesus Christ.

1

God's Protection Plan and Satan's Strategy

Covering

God's protection of His people is a theme that runs throughout the Bible from beginning to end. It is summed up in Psalm 91:1: "He who dwells in the shelter [the covered place] of the Most High will rest [abide, remain] in the shadow of the Almighty." For anyone who has made the Lord his dwelling place, the almighty God will be his protection, security and safety. God will stand between him and anything hostile.

Psalm 91 speaks of all kinds of terrors—terrors of the night, of diseases, of war. It refers to several of the ways the enemy seeks to destroy the child of God. But the central emphasis of this psalm is covering. It would be well worth taking time to read and meditate on the entirety of Psalm 91. Verse 4 tells us, "He will cover you with his feathers, and under his wings you will find refuge; his faithfulness will be your shield and rampart." And again, verses 9 and 10: "If you make the Most High your dwelling—even the LORD, who is my refuge—then no harm will befall you, no disaster will come near your tent." So we see that it is God's intention to provide protection for His people.

There are three Hebrew words used in the Old Testament for *covering*, with the following three meanings:

- to conceal or hide (this is the word most commonly used)
- to enclose or hedge in
- to protect or overlay

The word *covering* speaks of security, safety and protection.

The apostle Paul knew this! In his letter to the church in Ephesus, he instructs, "Put on the full armor of God so that you can take your stand against the devil's schemes" (Ephesians 6:11). Paul was telling us that no one who plays a part in extending God's eternal Kingdom is safe unless he knows how to be spiritually covered from head to foot.

In Christ

The little phrase, *in Christ,* is used over two hundred times in the New Testament. For instance, Paul wrote, "To all the saints *in Christ Jesus* at Philippi . . . " (Philippians 1:1, emphasis mine). The believer has been placed by the sovereign power of God *in* His Son. This is our covering under the new covenant.

As children of God, we are not just subjects of Christ. Our position in the sight of God is *in Christ.* If we are not in Christ, we are not God's children. To be Christians means that we are in Christ and He is in us. The two are synonymous.

When we believe, we believe *into* Christ. The Greek word that means "to believe in Christ" is a verb of action; it does not just refer to an academic belief. Our faith actually carries us into Him.

To be in Christ is to be covered by what He is: His holiness, His righteousness, His purity. All that He is in God covers us. So every time we read that we are "in Him," we are reading about our spiritual covering.

If you are in Christ, you can't be seen out of Him. When God looks at you, He sees Christ. Paul said, "Your life is now hidden with Christ in God" (Colossians 3:3). If something is hidden, it is lost to view and can be found only within the hiding place.

Where is your life? If I want to find you and you are in Christ, I must find Christ to be able to find you. This is a fundamental, foundational truth.

This truth means that when the enemy hunts for you he comes up against Christ. Christ is therefore your stronghold and fortress, your place of safety against the enemy. He is the rightful position of every child of God. In Christ there is absolute safety, absolute security, absolute protection.

The hymn writer Augustus Toplady expressed this in the last verse of his hymn, "A Debtor to Mercy Alone." He wrote:

> Yes, I to the end shall endure, as sure as the earnest is given;
> More happy, but not more secure, [are] the glorified spirits
> in heaven.

Toplady was saying that the people who had died as Christians and were now in glory were no safer or more secure than those of us here on earth. If we let that truth sink in, it will change our whole attitude toward Satan and the powers of darkness! We are *already* beyond the reach of the enemy if our life is hidden with Christ in God. And if we remain under this covering, we are as secure as those who are presently rejoicing in heaven.

When we are in Christ, the enemy can only get hold of us by dealing first with Christ. Yet the fact is that Christ has already dealt with Satan. So the dead in Christ are no more "in Christ" than we are. The enemy tries to blind us to this fact so that we think we are somehow second-class citizens of heaven. Not so! There is only one Church, the Church that is in Christ.

More Than Conquerors

Satan is more aware than we are that the Overcomer is the Lord Jesus Christ. The battle has already been fought and won. And so everyone who stays in Him must win as well. This scriptural statement is one that Satan cannot bear: "Thanks be to God, who always leads us in triumphal procession in Christ" (2 Corinthians 2:14). If Paul had said that God "sometimes leads us in triumphal procession in Christ," it would still have been a marvelous promise. But he said *always*. Christ has won the victory, and while we are abiding in Him, we are part of His victory procession.

Another great encouragement is found in 1 Corinthians 15:57–58: "Thanks be to God! He gives us the victory through our Lord Jesus Christ. Therefore, my dear brothers, stand firm. Let nothing move you. Always give yourselves fully to the work of the Lord." We are not only safe from harm but also positively victorious, and our work in Him will therefore be fruitful. His unassailable victory becomes ours and has an intensely practical nature.

Romans 8:37 tells us that we are "more than conquerors through him who loved us." Outside of Christ we are abject failures, but in Christ we are more than conquerors. Paul wrote to the believers in Ephesus, "God raised us up with Christ and seated us with him in the heavenly realms in Christ Jesus" (Ephesians 2:6). Paul saw that even the weakest and most ignorant believer, who nevertheless remains in Christ, can be absolutely victorious. However, the person who can write a theological tome but moves out of Christ will be totally defeated.

There is only one safe pace for us to be, and that is seated with Christ in heavenly places. Then we can overcome by the blood of the Lamb and by the word of our testimony (see Revelation 12:11). But we are bound to fail if we descend to earthly strategies, responding "in the flesh" and taking our old nature as the basis for our actions. Satan is the prince of this world, and everyone who is found on that ground is fair game for his attacks.

What Is Satan's Strategy?

Satan's great objective is to get us "uncovered," that is, out of our place of safety in the Lord. He knows that he cannot do anything against an individual or church when they are abiding under "the shadow of the Almighty" (Psalm 91:1), or to use New Testament terms, remaining "in Christ" (see John 15:1–8).

While we abide in Christ, Satan cannot reach us. He first meets with the authority, righteousness, power, mercy and grace of Christ, where he cannot stay. Therefore his central plan in his war against the saints is to entice us from our place of safety. He wants to expose us and bring us into a vulnerable position.

How does the enemy know about these things? Why is he so determined to "uncover" believers?

In Ezekiel we have one of the two references in the Bible that shed light upon Satan's origins. Ezekiel 28:14, 16 puts it this way:

> You were anointed as a guardian cherub,
>   for so I ordained you....
> Through your widespread trade
>   you were filled with violence,
>   and you sinned.
> So I drove you in disgrace from the mount of God,
>   and I expelled you, O guardian cherub,
>   from among the fiery stones.

The Revised Version translates the words *guardian cherub* as *covering cherub*. This seems to show that before the Fall the devil had a position that had to do with covering and was connected with the glory of God.

No wonder Satan understands the importance of covering for believers—even more than we do! His role was once to cover, but now it is to expose. For this reason, pulling us away from God's covering is his primary area of attack on people whose stories are recorded for us in the Bible. It is how he tempted the Lord Jesus. And it is how he tries to undermine us today.

Remember, though, that the Lord Jesus Christ is interceding for us. He sees our situation much better than we do. He understands us better than we understand ourselves. And He loves us with a love that is stronger than death.

Study questions:

1. What is the central emphasis of Psalm 91? What are some of the words used to describe this theme?
2. What does it mean to be "in Christ"?
3. How is it that we believers on earth are just as secure and victorious as those who are already in heaven?
4. What is Satan's primary strategy?
5. To what extent are you personally under the covering of God?

2

Covering in the Old Testament

This chapter provides a very brief overview of the subject of
covering in the Old Testament. Each heading deserves a major
study in its own right, but that is not possible here. However,
even as we quickly scan the Old Testament, we will begin to
grasp what a vital matter spiritual covering is in the sight of
God.

When speaking of Israel, Isaiah says:

> Before I was born the LORD called me;
>   from my birth he has made mention of my name.
> He made my mouth like a sharpened sword,
>   in the shadow of his hand he hid me;
> he made me into a polished arrow
>   and concealed me in his quiver.
>
> Isaiah 49:1–2

This is reminiscent of Toplady's hymn: "Rock of ages cleft for
me, let me hide myself in thee."

In Isaiah 51:16 we read, "I have put my words in your
mouth and covered you with the shadow of my hand—I who
set the heavens in place, who laid the foundations of the
earth, and who say to Zion, 'You are my people.'"

We have already seen this in Psalm 91:1, 4:

> He who dwells in the shelter of the Most High
>   will rest in the shadow of the Almighty....
> He will cover you with his feathers,
>   and under his wings you will find refuge.

Literally, the word *shelter* here means "covert" or "covered
place." Similarly, in Psalm 61:4 we read, "I long to dwell in

15

your tent forever and take refuge in the shadow of your wings."

Protection in Battle

Covering is also linked with the idea of God's protection in times of battle, as we read in Psalm 140:7: "O Sovereign LORD, my strong deliverer, who shields [covers] my head in the day of battle."

In Deuteronomy 33:12 we read of Benjamin: "Let the beloved of the LORD rest secure in him, for he shields him all day long, and the one the LORD loves rests between his shoulders."

The Work of Christ

In Isaiah 61:10 we begin to see the link between covering and the work of the Lord Jesus:

> I delight greatly in the LORD;
>   my soul rejoices in my God.
> For he has clothed me with garments of salvation
>   and arrayed me in a robe of righteousness.

The word *arrayed* here can also be translated as "covered."

Levitical Offerings

Most Christians today don't have even a remote understanding of the relevance of the Levitical offerings. Were these just part of the Old Testament law? No! The better we understand these offerings, the more we can see that they were all fulfilled by Christ, and they help us appreciate His finished work and its absolute relevance for every aspect of our lives today.

It is well worth taking the time to read about these offerings in Leviticus 1 through 7. There are five offerings mentioned in these chapters:

1. the burnt offering
2. the meal (or grain) offering
3. the peace (or fellowship) offering

4. the sin offering
5. the trespass (or guilt) offering

Christ has become every one of these offerings for us. He is the fivefold offering, or sacrifice. As such, He covers every single aspect of our relationship with God and with our fellow human beings. In other words, we are fully covered by the sacrifice of Jesus. Let's consider these offerings in more detail.

The Burnt Offering
The burnt offering was connected with service and worship to God. Some think that all you have to do is to give your life to God and fling yourself into His work. Yet that is the surest way to become uncovered!

This offering of an unblemished male was completely burned up. The whole thing had to be consumed by fire. In the same way, the farther and deeper we go in serving God, the more we must plead the covering of the Lord Jesus Christ as our burnt offering. Our service will never be acceptable to God apart from Christ.

The Meal Offering
The meal, or grain, offering, made up of fine flour mixed with salt, was always mixed with the other offerings. It speaks of our humanity. This offering was taken together with incense and oil and burned as a memorial on the altar.

Some Christians try so hard to be spiritual that they forget that they are human! But Jesus' perfect humanity shone through Him, even when God was most revealed in Him. He was offered *as a human being* for us. Jesus is the One who can bring righteous humanity into our lives as we accept His sacrifice and covering.

The Peace Offering
The peace, or fellowship, offering is the one offering in which everyone shared: first the priests, then the Levites and finally the people. Like the other offerings, it produced an aroma that was pleasing to God. It speaks of peace between us and God, as well as of peace between us and our brothers and sisters. We share in it together.

Do you know Christ as your fellowship offering? Relationships within the Church are constantly subjected to pressure. Our enemy is often breathing insinuations into our ears about one another. It is in his interest to strain relationships between believers to their breaking points.

Beware of depending solely on your natural affinities for someone else. Some of us think, *We get along so well, we will never fight!* Yet when the devil gets to work, even the dearest natural relationships can be pushed to their breaking points. This can be seen in what were once good Christian marriages, but which have fallen apart because Christ was not relied on to maintain the relationship.

Jesus Christ was our peace offering. His sacrifice makes reconciliation and true fellowship possible. He is our unity. We don't have to try to make our opinions the same. Rather, we must hold to the oneness of Christ, made available to us through the offering of Himself once and for all.

The Sin Offering

The sin offering is perhaps the most clearly understood by believers. Most of us are aware that we sin and fall short of God's standards. The sin offering covers both our sins of omission and commission (see Leviticus 5:1–4).

Blood was shed for the forgiveness of sins, and this offering was described as "most holy." This sacrifice was accompanied by confession of sin (Leviticus 5:5).

Jesus Christ died as our sin offering. There is no other way that we can atone for our sins. As we read in Ephesians 1:7, "In him we have redemption through his blood, the forgiveness of sins, in accordance with the riches of God's grace."

Our very redemption, or salvation, comes through the blood shed by Jesus Christ at Calvary. Was there ever a more sacred moment in history?

Each time we celebrate the breaking of bread in a Communion service, we are reminded that Jesus died for our sins. As we gather around the Lord's Table, we are reminded of these eternal truths and so are the powers and principalities that are looking on. However simply it is celebrated, Communion is most holy and should always be treated with reverence.

The Trespass Offering

The trespass, or guilt, offering was made when a person sinned unintentionally. We find many Christians today who assume that God won't hold them responsible for doing something they didn't understand to be sin. But that is not true!

Sin is sin, whether we know it to be sin or not. We all sin at times without realizing it, but this is what the trespass offering was created for. God passes over sin like this because Jesus was our guilt offering, not because we didn't realize we were doing something wrong. Notice that in the Old Testament the guilt offering was accompanied by acts of restitution (see Leviticus 5:16; 6:1–5).

In Summary

We have seen that Christ is our fivefold offering and covering. God has given us a salvation so perfect and complete that not a single line of attack from Satan need succeed.

The provision is there in Christ. But we do need to understand it and appropriate it. We must learn to pray with wisdom and persistence. We need to discern when to take the Lord Jesus as our peace offering, as our sin offering and so on. And it is only by the anointing of God that we can know these things.

As the devil draws near we must come under God's covering. If we are truly alive to the Spirit of God, we will know in our spirit what is happening and also know which specific aspect of the sacrifice of Christ is the answer. If, instead, we tackle the problem in the flesh, we will always make things worse instead of better. Much often needs to be accomplished "behind the scenes."

Leaders in our churches must learn how to appropriate Christ as our fivefold offering and plead Him for the whole of the body, especially for those who don't understand how to do this for themselves. Better still, they should teach their congregations about the covering provided for us in Christ, so that all Christians can learn to become more effective in countering the wiles of the enemy.

When Job's friends angered the Lord through some things they said, He told them to go and ask Job to pray for them. It was Job who had to ask God's forgiveness for his friends, and when he prayed, God did forgive them.

Similarly, when the children of Israel murmured against the Lord, God told Moses that He was going to destroy them. But Moses reminded God that He had brought them out of Egypt for a purpose, as a testimony of His power. Then the Lord told Moses to pray for the people, and because of those prayers, they were forgiven and spared destruction.

How we need leaders in the church today who will pray for their people when they have sinned! We are all prone to act in the flesh. But if we will simply remember these fivefold offerings, we will understand that there is another way. Even people who should have been struck down under the judgment of God have been kept safe by the secret prayers of their friends.

Study questions:

1. In what ways is the idea of covering found in the Old Testament?

2. How does the Old Testament foreshadow Christ's sacrifice for us?

3. Why are the Levitical offerings significant, even for us today?

4. How is Jesus our "fivefold offering"?

5. Have you understood, and are you appropriating, the covering and provision of Christ?

3

Covering in the New Testament

In the New Testament, there are three fundamental aspects of covering in Christ.

The Name of the Lord

We will start our study of spiritual covering in the New Testament by looking at John 14:13–14: "I will do whatever you ask in my name, so that the Son may bring glory to the Father. You may ask me for anything in my name, and I will do it." This is an astounding statement! What could Jesus have meant by it? He certainly didn't mean that we should just carelessly tack words like "in the name of the Lord Jesus Christ" on to the end of any prayer, like a little code that will produce a miracle.

Many Christians seem to think that the name of Jesus works like a magic charm. Yet you can't use the name of Jesus like that. What is requested in your prayer must be true and real and, above all, in the will of the Father. When that happens, you can take the name of Jesus on your lips and all hell will shake. But this will not happen otherwise.

What does the phrase *in the name of Jesus* really mean? It means that you are *in Him!*

The parts of my body are all *in* Lance Lambert. They are no one else's. Each of them can speak and act in my name.

When Jesus said, "I will do whatever you ask the Father in my name," what did He really mean? I believe He was teaching us that when we are in Christ we approach the Father *in Him*. In this position, we can simply say, "Father, we are not approaching You in our own merit—we are coming in Your Son."

21

We are in Him. We have a right to use His name. We read in Colossians 3:17, "Whatever you do, whether in word or deed, do it all in the name of the Lord Jesus." That is our position and privilege. It does not just apply to our prayer life. It means that as we abide in Him we do everything from a covered position.

So we should not separate the "spiritual" and "secular" sides of our lives. We cannot live a godly life while at a church meeting and an ungodly life at home or in our leisure pursuits. That is impossible. You are either *in* Christ, or you are *out* of Him. If God has put you in Him, you should not be doing anything outside of Him. Proverbs 18:10 says, "The name of the LORD is a strong tower; the righteous run to it and are safe." That is where we are meant to be as Christians: in the Strong Tower, which is our Lord Jesus Christ.

The Blood of Christ

What does it mean when we speak of Christ's blood? First John 1:7 says this: "If we walk in the light, as he is in the light, we have fellowship with one another, and the blood of Jesus, his Son, purifies us from all sin." Note the word *if* at the beginning of this verse. *If* we don't walk in the light with God and with one another, then the blood of Jesus Christ cannot continue to cleanse us.

We see this again in verse 9: "If we confess our sins, he is faithful and just and will forgive us our sins." There must be confession! The word *confess* means "to say the same thing." Confession is to recognize what God calls something and to call it the same. If God says that something is sin, then we must also say it is sin! If God says, "That was disobedient," then we must agree, "Lord, I was disobedient."

I know people who have been through terrible experiences and were severely attacked by the enemy. They have come to me, saying, "I don't understand it! I repeated the phrase again and again, 'the blood of Jesus, the blood of Jesus.'" But you can't appropriate the blood of Jesus while remaining in disobedience.

If Satan knows that he has a foothold in your life but you are reciting, "the blood of Jesus," Satan will just laugh! What you must do is to sort out the matter with confession and, if necessary, restitution. Then when Satan comes, you can say, "It is put under the blood of the Lamb" and have peace in your conscience.

You cannot be unreal in this matter. The invisible world around us sees the reality of things. You can't take Satan in or fool him by glibly referring to the blood of Jesus.

The blood of Christ speaks of peace, of immediate access to God, of victory. The blood also speaks of life, because the life is in the blood. Satan knows that his defeat took place in the shedding of blood, as we read in Revelation 12:10–11:

> The accuser of our brothers,
>> who accuses them before our God day and night,
>> has been hurled down.
> They overcame him
>> by the blood of the Lamb
>> and by the word of their testimony;
> they did not love their lives so much
>> as to shrink from death.

We can learn something more from the Old Testament here. The description of the Passover is given in Exodus 12:13, in which God said, "When I see the blood, I will pass over you." The power of Egypt and of Pharaoh, and the power of unseen forces, was broken that night by the blood of the lamb. The Egyptians were visited by the angel of death, while the Hebrews who had lamb's blood on the doorposts of their houses were passed over.

God sees the blood of His Son upon everyone who has been saved by His grace. It is this blood that covers and protects us. But it is possible to come out from under that covering, in ways that will be spelled out later.

The Righteousness of Christ

When we are in Christ, we can speak and act in His name, we are cleansed by His blood and we are robed in His righteousness. As Paul says in Philippians 3:9, "Not having a righteousness of my own that comes from the law, but that which is through faith in Christ—the righteousness that comes from God and is by faith." Or he says in 2 Corinthians 5:21, "God made him who had no sin to be sin for us, so that in him we might become the righteousness of God." Notice the words *in him* in this verse. When God places me in Him, I am made righteous, justified, acquitted and covered. We are in His righteousness. This is the garment of salvation referred to in Isaiah 61. Do you wear it? Or do you wear the spotted garments of your own good deeds?

Do you come to worship God, to the wedding feast, without this garment covering you? Christ has provided a robe of righteousness in which we can approach God. When He sees that robe, He will say, "You are all beautiful, my love!"

Some people are shocked that the Lord would say, "I can't find anything wrong in you." Because they don't know how to put on the robe of righteousness, they suffer from depression, and ultimately from enemy oppression. Although they have been saved by the grace of God, they disregard the garment of salvation and try to please God in their own strength.

Abiding in Christ

When the Lord Jesus knew that He was living in the last days of His life, He took great pain to teach the disciples one thing. The phrase He repeated over and over again was "Abide in me!"

Look at John 14–16. Jesus wanted His disciples to know that their only place of safety and fruitfulness could be found when they were abiding in Him.

To abide simply means to remain, stay, continue or dwell. You don't have to fight in order to abide under a spiritual covering. All you have to do is to stay where God has put you.

Where has God put you? In Christ. Stay there, and if you should happen to ever leave, return immediately. Whatever the cost, get back!

The Armor of God

Another New Testament picture of our being hidden in Christ is that of armor. Armor is the clothing that men would put on when they needed protection against an enemy in battle.

Paul encourages us with these words found in Ephesians 6:11–12, 14–17:

> Put on the full armor of God so that you can take your stand against the devil's schemes. For our struggle is not against flesh and blood, but against the rulers, against the authorities, against the powers of this dark world and against the spiritual forces of evil in the heavenly realms.... Stand firm then, with the belt of truth buckled around your waist, with the breast-plate of righteousness in place, and with your feet fitted with the readiness that comes from the gospel of peace. In addition to all this, take up the shield of faith, with which you can extinguish all the flaming arrows of the evil one. Take the helmet of salvation and the sword of the Spirit, which is the word of God.

In this famous passage, Paul tells us to put on the whole armor of God. There is no point in just putting on a few pieces and leaving other pieces off. That is exactly where the enemy will attack us!

Do you know the Lord Jesus as your Helmet of Salvation? Or are there times when your mind is attacked because you aren't wearing the helmet? The mind can be our most vulnerable area of attack.

Do you know Christ as your Truth? This means having our lives centered in honesty and reality. If there is any unreality, our lives won't hold together.

The breastplate of righteousness, or integrity, should be protecting our hearts. Christ alone is our righteousness—we can't trust in our own good deeds.

Our feet should be shod with the gospel of peace. We can't walk in the ways of God without knowing Christ as our peace. It is this peace that will rule, or arbitrate, in our hearts (see Colossians 3:15), that will "guide you in the decisions you make" (TEV). You will know which way to go when you follow the peace of Christ.

Do you know Christ as your Shield of Faith? We carry the shield in front of us and hide behind it when the fiery darts of the enemy come.

Ephesians 6:13 tells us why we must put on each piece of God's armor: "Therefore put on the full armor of God, so that when the day of evil comes, you may be able to stand your ground, and after you have done everything, to stand." This is really another way of telling us to abide in Christ! Having done everything, we are not required to march another hundred miles. No—this battle is won by abiding. Christ already won the victory on the cross, and it only needs to be ratified. We win when we stand in Christ. As we remain in Him, the victory is registered first in heavenly places and then on the earth.

The truths expressed in the New Testament make the Old Testament pictures and symbols all the more meaningful. Christ is our Fortress, Stronghold and Tower. It is His wings under which we find shelter. He is our Shield and Buckler. He is the Rock in whom we take refuge. He is our place of sanctuary and our hiding place.

Study questions:

1. What does the phrase *in the name of Jesus* really mean?
2. Why is the protection of the blood of Christ linked to our obedience?
3. How do we wear the robe of Christ's righteousness?
4. What does it mean to abide *in Christ?*
5. Are you wearing every piece of the armor of God? If not, what are you lacking?

4

How the Enemy Has Attacked Us in the Past

The stories recorded in the Bible have been given to us for our instruction and education, and we must learn from them as much as possible about covering. We will only be able to examine the most obvious examples.

Old Testament Examples

Adam and Eve (Genesis 3:7, 21)

When Adam and Eve first sinned against God, they were filled with shame and used fig leaves to cover their bodies.

Many believers try to sew together their own version of fig leaves as garments in which to come before God. We are always trying to present our good works to please Him. These "fig leaves" may look attractive and durable to us, but it is only blood that can cover us in God's sight. Only the righteousness of Jesus Christ matters.

Noah (Genesis 6–8)

When the flood came to engulf the earth in Noah's day, the Ark was the only thing that could save him and the rest of his family who took shelter inside. Everywhere else the judgment and curse of God were found, but inside the Ark were safety and shelter.

The Ark enclosed, or covered, everyone inside so that they were completely hidden, except for the one window that looked up toward heaven. The Ark preserved them from an old creation that was under the wrath of God, and it brought them securely to new life.

Christ is God's Ark for us, keeping us alive and safe within.

Many Christians seem to know nothing but death and its encroachments of heaviness, bondage, limitation, weakness and corruption. But in Christ our soul is kept in life, praise, freedom, fullness, power and wholeness. In Him God preserves us and provides for us.

In his old age, Noah became uncovered through drunkenness (see Genesis 9:20–27). His two older sons, Shem and Japheth, were blessed for covering their father's nakedness. As we read in Proverbs 10:12, "Love covers over all wrongs."

Farther in the story, Noah's youngest son, Ham, received a curse because he treated his father's shame lightly. By gloating over another person's fall or gossiping about it carelessly, we become vulnerable to the enemy, and in this way we too can become uncovered.

Abraham (Genesis 12:1–2, 10–20; 16:1–4)
Even someone with the spiritual stature of Abraham could become uncovered. He was tempted by Satan to venture outside of the will of God. When he stayed within the land of Israel, he had absolute safety and provision, but when he went to Egypt, he got himself into trouble.

Interestingly, it was through his wife's maid, Hagar, who was herself an Egyptian, that Abraham came to grief another time. By not trusting God for the fulfillment of His promise, Abraham departed from the covering that God had provided for him. As a result, Ishmael was born, and the family tensions between Ishmael and Isaac exist to this day.

Miriam and Aaron (Numbers 12:1–15)
Aaron was a godly man, and Miriam was a prophetess—both had been used greatly by God. But when they spoke against Moses, God rebuked them in anger, even causing Miriam to contract leprosy. Their words and attitudes had uncovered them.

Aaron recognized the sin that they had "so foolishly committed" and entreated Moses to pray for healing. Their sin had been to criticize the Lord's anointed one. In challenging Moses, they had challenged God Himself.

Many believers have spoken against an anointed minister of God or the order that God has instituted and so have become unclean. It is a terrible place in which to be, unless there is repentance.

The Spies in Canaan (Numbers 13:1–14:4)

The men whom Moses sent to explore the land of Canaan let go of their spiritual protection through their disbelief. They recognized that Canaan was a land of milk and honey, as God had promised, but they allowed themselves to be ruled by their fear. Their bad report caused the people to grumble against God and seek to turn back to Egypt.

Although there were enemies to be overcome, those who believed that victory was impossible ended up dying in the wilderness. But those who maintained their faith were covered by God's protection and lived to possess the Promised Land.

Korah and His Followers (Numbers 16:1–35)

Korah was a Levite—one who ministered to the Lord in the Tabernacle—who rose up against Moses together with two hundred fifty other leaders of the Israelite community. They "became insolent" and came as a group to oppose Moses. The root of their problem was jealousy and ambition. It took them out from under God's protection and brought them to a place of judgment and death.

In the Church today there are people who are status conscious, people who want to have a title or to feel that they have "arrived." What comes from earthly ambition will always get swallowed up by the earth, destroyed by fire.

Korah was absolutely convinced of the rightness of his position, even when judgment was imminent. Thinking we are right is no excuse. This sin is common in the Church, and we can be contradicting the Lord without even knowing it. Korah and his followers put forth their case very convincingly, so that others became partakers of their sin, and with the sin, the judgment. If you fail to disassociate yourself from things that you know in your spirit are wrong, you will also become uncovered and subject to the same judgment.

Achan (Joshua 7:1–26)

After Joshua's major victory at Jericho, the Israelites were routed in the comparatively minor region of Ai. Joshua tore his clothes and fell down before the Ark of the Lord along with the elders of Israel to seek the cause. The Lord then said:

> Israel has sinned; they have violated my covenant, which I commanded them to keep. They have taken some of the devoted things; they have stolen, they have lied, they have put them with their own possessions. That is why the Israelites cannot stand against their enemies; they turn their backs and run because they have been made liable to destruction. I will not be with you any more unless you destroy whatever among you is devoted to destruction.
>
> Joshua 7:11–12

Achan was revealed to have taken forbidden things from the plunder of Jericho. By hiding these in his tent and trying to deceive God and the leaders of Israel, he had uncovered not only himself but the whole of Israel. His punishment was to be stoned to death.

Uzzah (2 Samuel 6:1–11)
On the great occasion when the Ark of the Lord was being brought to Jerusalem, it was set on a cart instead of being carried by poles, as was specified in Exodus 25:12–16. Because of this act of disobedience, the Ark was at risk when the oxen stumbled, and Uzzah took hold of it in order to stabilize it. The Bible tells us that "the Lord's anger burned against Uzzah because of his irreverent act," and he was struck down and died.

God never judges anyone without a cause. The Ark of the covenant was a most holy thing, yet it was being treated casually and carelessly. Disobedience and a lack of respect for the things of God led to Uzzah's uncovering.

Job and His Friends
When Job was afflicted terribly with disaster and disease, his friends came to comfort him. Yet despite their concern and apparent wisdom, they did not have the mind of God about Job's condition. By speaking out of place and accusing Job of wrongdoing, they influenced Job also to speak foolishly. Thus they all became "uncovered" before God.

When the Lord questioned Job, he had no answers. Job realized that he had spoken beyond his understanding. He bowed before God, and God restored him. God was displeased with Job's friends because of their sermons, until sacrifices were offered and Job prayed for them.

We also must beware of getting uncovered by giving "helpful advice" to a person who is under the dealings of God. Sometimes there are inexplicable problems that God allows. When a trial is brought through the hand of God, we are absolutely safe, and the trial will ultimately work His glory in our lives.

Jesus' Temptation (Matthew 4)

We read in the New Testament how Jesus was tempted in three ways by the devil. Each time, Satan used the very words of Scripture to try to entice Jesus into doing something outside of the will of the Father for Him.

First, the devil tempted Jesus to turn stones into bread. We know that Jesus could have done this—after all, He later fed thousands of people with just a few loaves of bread and fish. In the case of His temptation, He had a legitimate need for food, as He had just fasted for forty days and was certainly very hungry.

But Jesus knew that He had no direction from God the Father to turn those stones into bread. He knew that He was to live instead "on every word that comes from the mouth of God." The devil's objective was to get Jesus to act independently from God. Although turning stones into bread would have been a miracle of the first order, seemingly expressing faith, it would have immediately made Jesus vulnerable to Satan's schemes.

Secondly, the devil took Jesus up onto a high pinnacle of the Temple and invited Him to cast Himself down to prove to the world that He was the Messiah. Satan even quoted Psalm 91, which speaks of God's protection:

> For he will command his angels concerning you
> > to guard you in all your ways;
> they will lift you up in their hands,
> > so that you will not strike your foot against a stone.
> > > > > > > > > > Verses 11–12

Again, this might seem to have been a wonderful thing for Jesus to do. The devil knew very well that it was possible for

Him, but Satan's goal was to entice Jesus to act apart from His Father. This would have taken Him outside of God's covering and protection.

The final temptation in the wilderness was for Jesus to worship and serve Satan instead of God. The devil promised as a reward "all the kingdoms of the world and their splendor." If he could have trapped Jesus into idolatry, as he has done with countless numbers before and since, then the Lord would have been defeated.

But Jesus gave no room to the enemy, and He commanded with the words of Deuteronomy 6:16, "Away from me, Satan! For it is written, 'Worship the Lord your God, and serve him only.'"

What rejoicing there must have been in heaven at that moment! And as the devil temporarily departed, angels came to minister to Jesus.

Yes, the Lord Jesus knew what it was like to be tempted by the devil, and we can be sure that this temptation continued throughout His life. The prayer He taught His disciples to pray came out of His own experience: "And lead us not into temptation, but deliver us from the evil one" (Matthew 6:13). This is how the Good News Bible translates the same verse: "Do not bring us to hard testing, but keep us safe from the evil one." Very few Christians consider the meaning of this prayer. The Lord's Prayer is that God would preserve us, save us from situations in which we might fall and become uncovered, for then the enemy would be able to get hold of us.

Do we pray this prayer enough? Jesus knew the force and cunning of the enemy, and He was trying to make His disciples aware of the danger. Every day of our lives, we should pray as the Lord taught us and not take our safety and victory for granted.

Study questions:

1. What is many Christians' modern equivalent of Adam and Eve's fig leaves?
2. How is Noah's Ark significant for us today?

3. Explain how Noah, Abraham, Miriam and Aaron, the spies in Canaan, Korah, Achan, Uzzah and Job and his friends all departed from God's covering in their lives.
4. In what way did the devil try to entice Jesus away from the Father's will for Him?
5. Do any of these examples have meaning for you personally? Are you praying for God's protection from the evil one?

5

How the Enemy Attacks Us Now

As we have already seen, the enemy's main strategy is to draw us out of our place of safety, where we are "hidden with Christ in God."

The Word of God clearly promises that we are in this place of safety when we abide in Christ. Yet, all around us, we can see spiritual casualties—and we ourselves are sometimes among those casualties.

It is bad enough to be knocked down temporarily, but we all know of people who once ran a good race as Christians but now are nowhere to be found. This state of being a casualty of the faith always begins with uncovering. Let's carefully consider how this happens.

The enemy knows that a frontal attack often doesn't work, so his strategy is to subtly entice us. He does this through trickery and deceit. He pretends to be an angel of light— a minister of righteousness—to lure us out from our position in Christ.

The devil is rather like a chameleon, the little lizard that is able to change its color according to its surroundings. Satan watches us closely to find out the weaknesses in our temperament, background or present circumstances. Then he moves in subtly, camouflaging himself so that we often are unaware that he is even at work.

Most of us think that we are immune from the treachery of the devil. We hardly think ourselves to be in danger. But the apostle Peter warns us, "Be self-controlled and alert. Your enemy the devil prowls around like a roaring lion looking for someone to devour" (1 Peter 5:8). While we are in Christ, we are in a place of absolute victory, and the devil cannot harm or devour us. But once we come out from under the Lord's covering, our hungry enemy will pounce.

How Satan Tempts Us out of Our Place of Safety

Not Walking in the Light

> God is light; in him there is no darkness at all. If we claim to have fellowship with him yet walk in the darkness, we lie and do not live by the truth. But if we walk in the light, as he is in the light, we have fellowship with one another, and the blood of Jesus, his Son, purifies us from all sin.
>
> 1 John 1:5–7

It is by Jesus' blood alone that our sins are covered. Yet to continue to be covered by His blood, we must walk in the light of God. We must open our whole lives to the searchlight of the Holy Spirit. This happens as we saturate ourselves in the Scriptures, because we cannot trust our own subjective interpretations of good and evil.

The way we walk farther into the light is to obey the light that God has already given us. If the Lord points His finger toward something in our lives and we say no, He will point it out again and perhaps a third time. However, if we keep rejecting His guidance, darkness will come upon us. We can carry on singing hymns and worship songs, reading the Bible and apparently living out our faith full steam, but those with discernment will know that something is wrong.

When we are not walking in the light, our fellowship with God is broken. But if we continue to deceive ourselves into thinking that all is well, we will move into spiritual bondage.

The apostle John had this to say: "If we claim to be without sin, we deceive ourselves and the truth is not in us" (1 John 1:8).

An Unforgiving Spirit

There is a part of the Lord's Prayer that says: "Forgive us our debts [sins], as we also have forgiven our debtors [those who have sinned against us]" (Matthew 6:12). Do we really understand the implications of praying this prayer?

When we pray this, we are actually asking God not to forgive us if we haven't forgiven someone else! It is a sobering thought indeed that if there is someone whom we cannot forgive, whether dead or alive, we ourselves will not be forgiven by God.

In the story of the two debtors in Matthew 18:21–35, the servant who had been forgiven an enormous sum refused to forgive his fellow servant. The master spoke severely to the unforgiving man and turned him over to the jailors. At the end of the story, Jesus commented, "This is how my heavenly Father will treat each of you unless you forgive your brother from your heart" (verse 35).

Some examples of people whom we might have particular difficulty forgiving include our parents, children, other relatives, bosses, neighbors or even other Christians. Many people harbor deep-seated feelings of unforgiveness because of an incident that took place in the past—and this becomes a stumbling block. But waiting until they *feel* like forgiving before extending forgiveness is a mistake—forgiveness must be an act of the will.

Some people who have been helped by deliverance ministry for demonic issues seem to relapse. Very quickly they fall back into the same bondage and return into darkness. Often at the root of the problem is the simple fact that they have not forgiven someone. Until they forgive, they will never truly be free.

We need a revelation of how much God has forgiven us, so that we in turn will forgive others. Without this forgiving spirit, we cannot be "hidden with Christ in God."

An Untamed Tongue

> Brothers, do not slander one another. Anyone who speaks against his brother or judges him speaks against the law and judges it. When you judge the law, you are not keeping it, but sitting in judgment on it. There is only one Lawgiver and Judge, the one who is able to save and destroy. But you—who are you to judge your neighbor?

This short passage from James 4:11–12 should be read in the light of Galatians 5:15, which says, "If you keep on biting and devouring each other, watch out or you will be destroyed by each other."

Can a Christian be destroyed? The answer must be yes or Paul would not have warned against it! By indulging in idle gossip, talebearing and criticizing, we put ourselves in danger of being consumed. The words we speak can come back on us like a boomerang.

How many believers do you hear cursing themselves with their own lips? Foolish talk about our health, our finances or our very future can give the enemy grounds to attack us. Some Christians foolishly say, "I'll probably get cancer—it runs in my family." Or, "If one more thing goes wrong, I'll go crazy!" Or, "No matter how much I earn, we'll never make ends meet." Or, "I'd rather die than lose him." Or simply, "I wish I were dead!"

Our own tongues can bring a curse upon us. Such words need to be confessed as sin and repented of. As we seek and receive God's forgiveness, the power of our disabling, harmful words can be revoked.

God wants to tame our tongues, and He is the only One who can do it. He can help us cope with the inner frustrations that so often result in our unwise words. He can deal with our anger or our critical nature. He wants to get at the source of the problem, because "out of the overflow of the heart the mouth speaks" (Matthew 12:34).

Pride

Pride is a primary cause of uncovering, and it also underlies many other causes of problems.

Let's look again at Ezekiel 28:17: "Your heart became proud on account of your beauty, and you corrupted your wisdom because of your splendor." Pride always goes before a fall, and Satan fell through pride.

The other passage in Scripture that addresses Satan's fall is found in Isaiah 14: "I will raise my throne above the stars [throne] of God ... I will make myself like the Most High" (verses 13–14). It was pride that caused the covering angel, Lucifer, to fall from heaven and be stripped of his role. Pride unfailingly brings us into a position of uncovering.

In James 4:6–7 we read, " 'God opposes the proud but gives grace to the humble.' Submit yourselves, then, to God. Resist the devil, and he will flee from you." When pride is in us, even if we are not conscious of it, we place ourselves in opposition to God. Instead of being our protector, He is standing against us. But if we submit ourselves to God, then we can resist the devil, and he will flee from us.

In Proverbs 16:18 we read, "Pride goes before destruction, a haughty spirit before a fall." Chapter 18:12 tells us, "Before his downfall a man's heart is proud, but humility comes before honor." Pride or hurt pride is so often the cause of believers' not walking in the light. It lies at the root of many of our unforgiving attitudes. In all these things we need to know the brokenness of the cross.

Pride is not only demonstrated in the way we interact with other people. We can be proud and arrogant in our dealings with God Himself. Some of us presumptuously think that we have a right to everything we want from God. Others think they can tell God what to do. But the Lord declares, "This is the one I esteem: he who is humble and contrite in spirit, and trembles at my word" (Isaiah 66:2).

Not Fearing the Lord

The fear of the Lord is something we don't hear much about in the twenty-first century. Many of us associate it with the Dark Ages. But God has not changed, and His power is no less a consuming fire than it ever was.

The more the Lord manifests Himself in and through us, the greater our reverence for Him will become. We begin to realize that we are dealing with a holy and mighty God. Hebrews 12:28–29 tells us to "worship God acceptably with reverence and awe, for our 'God is a consuming fire.'"

This theme runs through the Old Testament. In Psalm 19:9 we read, "The fear of the LORD is pure." It is unlike any fear that comes from the pit of hell and is unclean.

The fear of the Lord also is "enduring forever" (Psalm 19:9). Because God does not change, His awe-inspiring holiness and majesty remain the same. Our fear and reverence for God also brings something enduring and of lasting value into our lives.

Taking the Name of the Lord in Vain

The third of the Ten Commandments is this: "You shall not misuse the name of the LORD your God, for the LORD will not hold anyone guiltless who misuses his name" (Exodus 20:7). This is an abiding principle. To misuse or take the Lord's name in vain means to use it in a false or empty way, to make it common or drag it through the dirt. It is the opposite of how Jesus taught us to pray in the Lord's Prayer of Matthew 6:9: "Hallowed be your name." This use of God's name is to make it holy or to sanctify it.

Beware of using God's name in a manipulative way. The moment we do that, we become uncovered. Instead of the name of the Lord being a strong tower into which the righteous can run and be safe, our misuse of it causes us to be driven out, and our position becomes the exact opposite of a refuge.

Sometimes the name of Jesus is chanted like a Hindu mantra, with the devotee mindless of who He really is. Other people address the Lord Jesus in a way that discounts His divinity and purity. Blasphemous use of the words *God, Jesus* and *Christ* have become casual and accepted.

Be very careful, therefore, how you use the name of the Lord. It is not a charm or a way of gaining influence. It should not be spoken carelessly. The apostles who had once known Jesus in the flesh began, after His ascension, to speak of Him as Jesus Christ, or the Lord Jesus Christ, or Jesus our Lord.

Take a look at Malachi 3:16: "Those who feared the LORD talked with each other, and the LORD listened and heard. A scroll of remembrance was written in his presence concerning those who feared the LORD and honored his name." The people who feared the Lord also honored His name in their conversation. This was so precious to God that He even recorded what they had said!

Making Rash Promises
Making rash promises is another area of trouble into which our speech can draw us. In Mark 14:29–31 we read of how Peter fell into this trap:

> Peter declared, "Even if all fall away, I will not."
> "I tell you the truth," Jesus answered. "Today—yes, tonight—before the rooster crows twice you yourself will disown me three times."
> But Peter insisted emphatically, "Even if I have to die with you, I will never disown you." And all the others said the same.

Peter and the other disciples all expressed their intention never to deny Jesus. We read the result in a parallel passage, Luke 22:31: "Simon, Simon, Satan has asked to sift you [plural] as wheat. But I have prayed for you [singular], Simon, that your faith may not fail." Satan had gone before God to obtain permission to take the disciples. They had not recognized the truth of Jesus' words, and they had made rash vows based on their sense of their own steadfastness and human loyalty.

It was only the intercession of the Lord Jesus that resulted in an eventual glorious end for the disciples. He was praying for each personally by name, that their faith would not fail. Even though Peter denied the Lord, his faith ran deeper than his denial. He came through.

Ecclesiastes 5:2 warns us, "Do not be quick with your mouth, do not be hasty in your heart to utter anything before God." We should think through those things we vow to God and not make careless promises. Proverbs 20:25 reads, "It is a trap for a man to dedicate something rashly and only later to consider his vows." Often pride and complacency underlie such promises. It would be better not to make the vow in the first place.

Calling Satan Names

It is all too common these days for people to be abusive toward Satan. Of course, we are not to cower in corners, afraid of the enemy. The devil should be afraid of us! We can be bold because of the finished work of Christ.

Yes, we must resist the devil and all of his principalities and powers. We have the authority to cast out demons. But it is the way in which we do it that matters. Some believers speak any words that pop into their heads.

Jude warns us against behaving like some "godless men" (Jude 4), saying:

> In the very same way, these dreamers pollute their own bodies, reject authority and slander celestial beings. But even the archangel Michael, when he was disputing with the devil about the body of Moses, did not dare to bring a slanderous accusation against him, but said, "The Lord rebuke you!" Yet these men speak abusively against whatever they do not understand; and what things they do understand by instinct,

like unreasoning animals—these are the very things that destroy them.

Jude 8–10

These verses warn us not to speak against things we do not understand. My advice is never to call Satan names; keep to the terms used of him in the Bible. Don't make a joke about the devil or try to denigrate Satan.

Satan is a terrible reality. As Jude says, even Michael was careful and said, "The Lord rebuke you!" In these anti-authoritarian days, don't think you can say and do anything you like, even where Satan and his demonic forces are concerned. When dealing with evil spirits at any level, hide yourself in Christ. It is your place of both safety and authority.

Disobedience to the Will of God

Apart from following God's will as revealed in Scripture, we must be attentive to His voice speaking through the Holy Spirit. If God speaks to you, even on what seems to be a trivial matter, obey Him. Sometimes a tremendous amount rests on the smallest issues of obedience and disobedience.

King David became spiritually uncovered when he didn't go out to war with his men. Instead of heading the troops, he stayed at home, in disobedience to God. While in that vulnerable state, he was tempted by Satan when he went to the rooftop, saw Bathsheba and the idea of possessing her entered his mind. Later, to try to cover up his sin, he conceived the foul plan of killing her husband.

When David went up to the rooftop, he might have intended to pray or meditate, or to write a new song to God. But because he was out of the will of God, Satan was able to take advantage of this to try to destroy not only David but the people and work of God.

It is wonderful that the Spirit of the Lord brought David to repentance, and he eventually recorded his sorrow in the words of Psalm 51. He knew that he had been washed whiter than snow and Satan no longer had a hold over him because of his sin, despite how heinous it had been.

When we disobey God on a large or a small matter, the enemy often entices us into further sin, as he did with David.

Or, as in the story of the Prodigal Son, he tries to draw us away into the far country where we waste our life. When we persist in habitual or willful sin, we open ourselves to enemy attacks of every kind. Therefore Scripture says, "Do not be foolish, but understand what the Lord's will is" (Ephesians 5:17).

Part of understanding the will of the Lord is abiding in God's anointing. Look at 1 John 2:27:

> As for you, the anointing you received from him remains in you, and you do not need anyone to teach you. But as his anointing teaches you about all things and as that anointing is real, not counterfeit—just as it has taught you, remain in him.

As long as we heed the anointing, which tells us what is right and what is wrong, we are abiding in Christ. Yet the moment we make decisions and minister in our own wisdom and strength, we are leaving God's covering.

Whenever you hear that warning bell in your spirit, heed it!

Setting Aside God's Divine Order

It is particularly characteristic of the times in which we live, that the divine order is disregarded. Look at the principles of God's order in 1 Peter 2:13–3:7 and 5:1–8. It is not by chance that in the context of this letter, which talks about submission, we find Peter's warning about the devil's prowling about like a roaring lion.

God has a divine order for us: in our personal lives, in our family life, in our church, at work and in society. We need to beware of the spirit of the age, which under the guise of liberation will encourage us to stray from this divine order.

If a wife starts bossing her husband around, she becomes uncovered. If a husband is harsh and dishonoring to his wife instead of loving her as Christ loves His Church, he becomes uncovered too. If we speak disrespectfully of our employers or our governing officials, we also come out from under the shelter of God's protection.

In Summary

Satan has many ways in which he tries to lure us away from God's covering. Over many centuries, he has practiced his trickery and trained his demonic forces. Yet instead of heeding the solemn warnings in Scripture and being wary of the dangers, we are too often ignorant of Satan's devices and plans.

Some people say, "Before I even knew where I was, such-and-such happened!" Through lack of knowledge and wisdom, we can suddenly find ourselves outside of Christ. Bewildered Christians then ask, "Why me? Why did this happen?"

Some things do come by the permission of our sovereign God—we can learn about this from the life of Job. However, much of the trouble we experience in life is caused by our own actions when we leave God's covering.

Study questions:

1. Why are there so many spiritual casualties when it is possible to be safe in God?
2. What tactics does the devil use to lure us away from our position in Christ?
3. What does it mean to "walk in the light"?
4. How do pride, unforgiveness, careless speech, disobedience and other sins remove us from God's protection?
5. When you hear warning bells in your spirit, do you heed them?

6

The Enemy's Attack on the Church

Satan's objective is not only to draw the individual child of God outside of divine protection. His aim is also to cause the Church to be uncovered so that he can paralyze or even destroy it. There is evidence of this on every page of church history. Many works of God that began powerfully have ended up in absolute disarray.

We have only to look around us at the present church scene for evidence that the enemy is at work. So many groups are divided. Churches that started so well, with a desire to follow the Lord, are now weakened or even disbanded.

The root causes of churches becoming uncovered are basically the same as with individual believers. Particular problem areas are relationship problems, pride, a lack of reverence for God, presumptuous claims and the setting aside of divine order.

A church can become uncovered just as easily as an individual believer can, but the consequences can be even worse. Where there is no real love between believers, divisions will crop up. Where there is no fear of the Lord, deception can easily creep in.

Unforgiveness

We have already seen how unforgiveness can cause us to lose our own individual spiritual protection. This is certainly true in churches as well.

In 2 Corinthians 2:5–11, Paul urges believers to forgive someone who has caused grief to the fellowship in some way. He tells them to forgive "in order that Satan might not outwit us. For we are not unaware of his schemes" (verse 11). In the American Standard Version, this is translated, "that no advantage may be gained over us by Satan." Paul was aware of Satan's schemes, as we also must be.

Not Loving One Another

Satan will seek to bring discord between believers. When there are difficulties in relationships, things often become hidden and pushed under the carpet or buried. The people concerned are no longer walking in the light with one another, and this may cause them to avoid certain meetings or situations. This is a slippery slope into darkness, which can cause a church to become unfruitful.

Through this disruption of fellowship, the enemy has succeeded in drawing many away from Christ's protection. John wrote, "Anyone who claims to be in the light but hates his brother is still in the darkness. Whoever loves his brother lives in the light, and there is nothing in him to make him stumble" (1 John 2:9–10). If we don't love our brothers and sisters, we will stumble in the darkness created by our closed attitudes. This is one reason why so many believers fall.

Walking in love is particularly challenging when we are disappointed or betrayed by someone. But if we don't have fellowship with other believers, we are out of the spiritual covering God would have for us. It is an absolute law. The moment we no longer walk in love, that very moment we are being pushed out of our position in Christ. Let this sink in!

Lack of the Fear of God

At Pentecost, when the authority of the Lord was most evident, the reverence of God fell upon the people. We read in Acts 2:43, "Everyone was filled with awe." And this happened to the believers corporately.

When the Spirit of God is truly present, awe falls upon us. We begin to watch far more carefully the way we conduct ourselves, the way we behave, the things we say. This is not due to a cringing fear, but it is out of a respect, sensitivity and love for God. This fear of the Lord doesn't bring bondage but freedom. As with the early Church, we will be liberated to witness, worship and contribute to God's work.

Look briefly at the story of Ananias and Sapphira in Acts 5:1–11. Although they claimed they were giving all the proceeds from the sale of their property to the church, they were, in fact, keeping some of it back for themselves. Many of us have done something very similar—while blithely saying, "Lord, I give You everything," or singing, "All to Jesus I surrender."

Ananias and Sapphira thought that they were just dealing with people: Peter, the other apostles and the rest of the church. But Peter said, "You have not lied to men but to God" (Acts 5:4). They were committing perjury against the Holy Spirit, and they had no fear of the Lord. The result was death. Luke tells us, "Great fear seized the whole church and all who heard about these events" (verse 11).

Often in our dealings with one another, we don't recognize the Lord in our midst, and we become careless and arrogant. When we fail to fear God, there will come spiritual paralysis and bondage, or even death within whole church communities, until we put things right.

Taking God's Name in Vain

Some of us devalue the Lord's name, and this can become a habit even in church meetings. Some say, "The Lord has given me a word," when it was really our own thought. We tack the name of the Lord onto something to justify our course of action, often to justify ourselves in front of others. We use His name to impress other people or to get our own way in the church.

Scripture has harsh words for presumptuous prophets who claimed God's authority upon words He had not spoken. Look, for instance, at Deuteronomy 18:20–22 and Jeremiah 14:14–15.

In these days, when the Lord is speaking prophetically to His Church, we need to be careful to discern what is truly from Him and what is not. When we sense God is giving us a word for someone else, we should always say, "*I believe* the Lord is saying such and such ... please test this word." Our genuine mistakes are forgivable when our motives are pure.

An Untamed Tongue

James warns us that our speech is a danger area for us all:

> We all stumble in many ways. If anyone is never at fault in
> what he says, he is a perfect man, able to keep his whole body
> in check.... No man can tame the tongue. It is a restless evil,
> full of deadly poison. With the tongue we praise our Lord and
> Father, and with it we curse men, who have been made in
> God's likeness.
>
> James 3:2, 8–9

It is sobering that these words are addressed to the Church!
The very tongue with which we sing God's praises and pray is
the same tongue we use against one another. We contaminate
our fellowship by speaking unadvisedly against others.

Sometimes we listen to slander or gossip about another
believer, and because we have not disassociated ourselves
from what has been said, we become partakers in that sin.
Again, we become unclean and uncovered.

Sometimes people talk presumptuously about a missionary
society, church ministry or other group of believers. In our
arrogance, we are too often insensitive to the ways and
purposes of God. Sometimes we see His acts but don't understand His ways. So beware of what you say about a message
you have heard, about another person's testimony or about
a work of God, even if it does not make sense to you at that
time.

It is a grievous thing when there is slander within the
church, but you don't need to argue or defend yourself if
people criticize you for what you are doing. If you know you
are in the will of God, leave it to the Lord to deal with such
people. Proverbs 13:3 tells us, "He who guards his lips guards
his life, but he who speaks rashly will come to ruin." And
again, Proverbs 21:23 says, "He who guards his mouth and his
tongue keeps himself from calamity."

So, we need to guard our lips, tongue and mouth! We can
foolishly say things that can even be heard in hell. God hears
our conversations, and we also have an enemy who listens and
uses our words against us. Our own sin can provide an opening for him and take us out of our divine covering.

Disunity

One of the primary ways in which the enemy attacks the Church is by destroying our unity. The consequences are extremely serious. For a start, disunity reverses the promise of blessing found in Psalm 133:

> How good and pleasant it is
>   when brothers live together in unity!
> It is like precious oil poured on the head,
>   running down . . . on Aaron's beard,
>   down upon the collar of his robes.
> It is as if the dew of Hermon
>   were falling on Mount Zion.
> For there the LORD bestows his blessing,
>   even life for evermore.

Paul speaks very soberly in 1 Corinthians 11:17–18, 29–30:

> In the following directives I have no praise for you, for your meetings do more harm than good. In the first place, I hear that when you come together as a church, there are divisions among you, and to some extent I believe it.... For anyone who eats and drinks without recognizing the body of the Lord eats and drinks judgment upon himself. That is why many of you are weak and sick, and a number of you have fallen asleep.

The judgment of God, which was resulting in weakness, sickness and death, was in part due to disunity within the body. This is not something that we can excuse lightly.

We need to consider unity not only within local church bodies but also in the Church at large. If there is an attitude of competition or contempt of other churches, within our towns, cities, countries or even internationally, we will lose the favor of God. We need to show love to other Christians wherever they are and to whatever denomination or church they belong.

Pride

When a church becomes proud or begins to make presumptuous claims, you can be almost certain that it will start to crumble. If God does something special in your church or denomination, make sure that all the glory goes to Him.

It is vital that churches learn to heed the anointing of God. He will warn a church of danger, but we must obey and act. Because He is gracious, He will often speak twice or more on the same subject.

Disobedience and Sin

Sometimes when we come to a meeting, it feels "heavy" or "dark." The causes for this can be as simple as unwitting or unintentional sin. For example, someone may have talked or behaved unwisely, and because we are all bound together in one body, one person's sin affects the others. The invisible forces of evil can then come in like a flood.

In such a case we need to hold up the Lord Jesus Christ as a trespass offering. Immediately the disturbing atmosphere will shift. It does no good to just blame other human beings or the circumstances. If we start blaming people, then roots of bitterness can take hold.

A church may also become uncovered because they have set aside the divine order. Often members of the body of Christ become vulnerable to the attacks of the enemy because of unwise words they have spoken or bad attitudes they have had toward their church leaders. This doesn't just pertain to ministers or pastors. It is dangerous to override someone else's function in the body, however weak or insignificant that person may appear to be.

As we have seen, one of the sternest warnings in the New Testament comes when Paul chastises the church in Corinth. He says about their behavior at the Communion table, "When you come together, it is not the Lord's Supper you eat, for as you eat, each of you goes ahead without waiting for anybody else. One remains hungry, another gets drunk" (1 Corinthians 11:20–21).

This judgment on believers has to do with what the bread and wine symbolize. Individuals or groups in churches can lose their covering by partaking of the elements "in an unworthy manner" (verse 27). In this way they give the enemy an opening to attack. Paul warns that this was the cause of sickness and even death among believers.

John also speaks about "sin that leads to death" (1 John 5:16). We may need to consider this when our prayers are unanswered.

In 1 Corinthians 5, Paul tells leaders how to deal with immorality in the church. In an instance of sexual immorality, he advises:

> When you are assembled in the name of our Lord Jesus and I am with you in spirit, and the power of our Lord Jesus is present, hand this man over to Satan, so that the sinful nature [or that his body; the flesh] may be destroyed and his spirit saved on the day of the Lord.
>
> Verses 4–5

What a sobering message from Paul to the Church! He saw that uncovering of an extreme kind can lead to the physical destruction of the body, but it is done in order that the spirit may be saved.

If you have a church that began well but has floundered, consider the issues of covering. In that way you may "re-cover" the church, in more ways than one.

Those in leadership must learn to recognize when the church has strayed out of God's protection. They must teach their flock on these matters. And they must learn how to take Christ as their fivefold offering and plead Him for the whole Church!

Study questions:

1. What are the root causes of churches losing their spiritual protection? Why would Satan want to target the Church?
2. What did Paul warn the Church about as a consequence of unforgiveness?
3. In what way does careless talk, particularly about God's will, cause the Church to lose God's protection?
4. How does disunity affect churches and the purposes of God?
5. Is your church outside of God's covering? If so, what can you do about it?

7

How to Be Restored to a Place of Safety

There is no need whatsoever for us to lose our spiritual protection. We are encouraged in every way not to do so! Yet the fact is that most of us, along with our churches, do become uncovered at some point.

If the enemy has enticed you away from God's will, if you have said something unwise, if you are in darkness or if you have unresolved issues with someone else, then you have left your place of safety in Christ. Unless you deal with the problem, you will be in trouble.

There are five simple things to learn and remember when we find that we have become uncovered:

1. Take Immediate Action

Don't let the problem persist for minutes, let alone days, before you put things right. It only takes Satan a moment to gain an advantage when you are in such a condition. Just as many are saved or converted suddenly, so too deception can come suddenly. When you hear the gracious voice of the Spirit of God saying, "Put that right," do so at once.

Notice what Jesus said in the Sermon on the Mount about the urgency of sorting out sin:

> Settle matters quickly with your adversary who is taking you to court. Do it while you are still with him on the way, or he may hand you over to the judge, and the judge may hand you over to the officer, and you may be thrown into prison. I tell

you the truth, you will not get out until you have paid the last penny.

Matthew 5:25–26

Paul also tells us, "Do not let the sun go down while you are still angry, and do not give the devil a foothold" (Ephesians 4:26–27). When we follow God's instruction in these matters, we give room to Him and not to the enemy.

2. Acknowledge That You Are Uncovered

Don't make excuses! You need to be absolutely and strictly honest with yourself. Confess it, both in your heart and with your lips: "I said something I shouldn't have said," or "I did something that I shouldn't have done."

"Walk in the light, as he is in the light" (1 John 1:7). Don't reduce the light to grayness, to twilight, to dusk. When you come into the light, you will see things as they really are.

Confess your sin clearly and concisely. If you said something, retract the very words you said. Repentance is as much for the converted as for the unconverted. If we ask Him, the Holy Spirit will bring to our memory the exact point at which we became uncovered. He will give us the understanding and help that we need.

3. By Faith, Retake Your Divinely Given Position in Christ

However much the accuser says that your case is hopeless, by faith you must retake your position. This is the place that is yours through the finished work of Christ and the grace of God alone. Remember that you can't achieve this position by any good works or merit of your own.

Your basis for recovery is God's grace and the blood of Jesus. As Paul said:

> Don't you know that all of us who were baptized into Christ Jesus were baptized into his death? We were therefore buried with him through baptism into death in order that, just as Christ was raised from the dead through the glory of the Father, we too may live a new life.

> If we have been united with him like this in his death, we
> will certainly also be united with him in his resurrection. For
> we know that our old self was crucified with him so that the
> body of sin might be done away with, that we should no
> longer be slaves to sin.
>
> Romans 6:3–6

4. Put Right Whatever Is Wrong, Whatever the Cost

Sometimes this process can be very costly to our pride,
especially when it involves others or even the whole church.
But there is no "back door" when it comes to covering. It is
only when we are walking in the light that we have true
fellowship with one another. You will never regain your
position in Christ until you are prepared to humble yourself
and set things right.

Jesus told us:

> If you are offering your gift at the altar and there remember
> that your brother has something against you, leave your gift
> there in front of the altar. First go and be reconciled to your
> brother; then come and offer your gift.
>
> Matthew 5:23–24

If you have said or done something wrong and the only action
you take is to put it right with the Lord, sooner or later you will
fall again on the same issue. But if you have had to put the
thing right with other people, the lesson is burned into you. It
will be written indelibly on your heart. You will think twice
before you will go through that experience again!

5. Learn the Lesson

When you have become uncovered, there is always a cause. It
does not just happen without a reason. We must learn the
lesson so that we don't make the same mistake ever again. A
fool is not someone who makes a mistake but who makes the
same mistake again and again, refusing to learn.

We need to maintain a teachable spirit. It is much better
to learn how to stay covered than continually to have to

find our way back into God's protection. That is the way of progress.

Those who refuse either to recognize that they have become uncovered or to learn the lesson from their mistakes invariably go off course. We must learn to recognize our points of departure from the Lord. Then we must learn not to remain in a condition of danger one moment longer than we have become aware of it.

Christ as Intercessor and Mediator

We have already seen that when we are uncovered we are in terrible spiritual danger. The enemy and his host of demonic followers then have a legal right to successfully attack us. And that is why the Lord Jesus intercedes for us. No wonder Christians throughout the ages have written whole books on the intercession of the Lord Jesus Christ at the right hand of God!

When we begin to see the many ways in which we may lose God's protection, we realize what a precious and wonderful thing the intercession of Christ really is. He, more than any other, sees the danger, knows our frailty and weakness and prays with great power and authority for us.

The Lord Jesus doesn't just pray for us as individuals. His intercessory ministry reaches back before time and forward into the ages to come. He is praying for the fulfillment of God's purposes, for the preparation of His Bride, the Church. The scope of His intercession is wider than our finite minds can grasp.

How marvelous that the Lord intercedes for us rather than condemning us. Paul cried out in Romans 8:31–34:

> If God is for us, who can be against us? He who did not spare his own Son, but gave him up for us all—how will he not also, along with him, graciously give us all things? Who will bring any charge against those whom God has chosen? It is God who justifies. Who is he that condemns? Christ Jesus, who died— more than that, who was raised to life—is at the right hand of God and is also interceding for us.

God's desire is to save, not to condemn. Our salvation is

complete in Christ. The writer to the Hebrews said, "There-fore he is able to save completely those who come to God through him, because he always lives to intercede for them" (Hebrews 7:25). However terrible the circumstances, however difficult the situation or the personality, Christ is there interceding. He is no less an intercessor in the twenty-first century than He was in the first century. Earlier in Hebrews we read: "Because Jesus lives forever, he has a permanent priesthood" (7:24). His priesthood is the same yesterday, today and forever.

Jesus intercedes for us today. "He entered heaven itself, now to appear for us in God's presence" (Hebrews 9:24).

Before we can learn how to recover our right position in Christ, we must understand what the Lord Jesus feels for us and is doing for us. Read again that well-known passage in Hebrews 4:14–16:

> Therefore, since we have a great high priest who has gone through the heavens, Jesus the Son of God, let us hold firmly to the faith we profess. For we do not have a high priest who is unable to sympathize with our weaknesses, but we have one who has been tempted in every way, just as we are—yet was without sin. Let us then approach the throne of grace with confidence, so that we may receive mercy and find grace to help us in our time of need.

Don't stay away from God's mercy and throne of grace because you have sinned and become uncovered. Jesus is there to represent you to God (see Hebrews 5:10). He literally "re-presents" us.

Jesus knows us from the inside out. He is touched by the feelings of our worst sins and our smallest shortcomings. He knew what was in Peter, and He knows just as well what is in each one of us. He understands the inner workings of our minds, the complexities of our nature, our motives, our circumstances as well as our actions. And He is not judging us but interceding for us!

The Lord Jesus knows that the enemy would like to devour us, as a roaring lion. Therefore, He is praying for us: "My prayer is not that you take them out of the world but that you protect them from the evil one" (John 17:15). He also taught

His followers to pray, "Deliver us from the evil one" (Matthew 6:13). These are surely intimations of the kind of prayer that He is making for us right now.

Read again John 17 in which Jesus prayed first for Himself, then for His disciples and then for all believers. He spoke of protecting the disciples by the power of His name—that is, by the power of all that His name represents. He prayed, "I protected them and kept them safe by that name you gave me" (John 17:12).

If Jesus kept the disciples safe, won't He do the same for us? They were just like us, a mixed bunch who had both successes and failures. And even after Jesus' three years with them, He still said that He had kept them.

In this passage, Jesus also prayed for unity, saying to the Father: "I have given them the glory that you gave me, that they may be one as we are one: I in them and you in me. May they be brought to complete unity to let the world know that you sent me and have loved them even as you have loved me" (John 17:22–23).

It is as we abide in the Father, in the Son and in the Holy Spirit that we are able to maintain true unity with one another. Anything that divides or destroys that unity will cause uncovering. How serious this matter is, yet how easily it is discounted in the Church today.

We must remember that the basis of the Lord's intercession for us is that He has offered Himself as a living sacrifice once and for all. Just as through the Levitical offerings every part of the Jewish believer's life was covered, so every single part of our lives is covered by Christ's sacrifice: our worship, service, humanity, fellowship and sin.

In His self-offering, Jesus made provision for every one of us to become covered, to stay covered and to become covered again after we fall. This protection does not depend on our own zeal or devotion. It is founded on Christ's finished work alone. Even His intercessions for us today are based on that finished work.

At the end of the little book of Jude, we read, "To him who is able to keep you from falling and to present you before his glorious presence without fault and with great joy" (verse 24). The Amplified Bible expresses this verse in these words:

Now to him who is able to keep you without stumbling or slipping or falling, and to present you unblemished (blameless and faultless) before the presence of his glory—in triumphant joy and exultation—with unspeakable, ecstatic delight.

The sure and unshakable ways that Jesus keeps us blameless and spotless are through His own sacrifice and intercessions for us. As intercessor, He is also our mediator and advocate. John says, "If anybody does sin, we have one who speaks to the Father in our defense—Jesus Christ, the Righteous One. He is the atoning sacrifice for our sins, and not only for ours but also for the sins of the whole world" (1 John 2:1–2).

The apostle Paul had many faults. In both the Book of Acts and in his personal letters, we can see his humanity with its weaknesses. Yet in 2 Timothy 4:7, Paul wrote, "I have fought the good fight, I have finished the race, I have kept the faith." Paul could say that he had successfully finished his course; and the Lord Jesus can keep each one of us "on course" as well.

Study questions:

1. What did Jesus say about the urgency of dealing with the sin in our lives?
2. Explain the importance of confession.
3. How do we resume our position in Christ?
4. How does Jesus Himself keep us blameless and protected?
5. In what way do you need to personally respond to this message?

8

The Mystery of Covering and God's Glory

The subject of covering is like an iceberg—very little is obvious and easily discerned; a vast amount of the whole matter lies hidden beneath the surface. All that is possible in a small book like this is to whet your appetite to study the topic further.

We need an inquiring and sensitive spirit in our walk with God. If the fear of the Lord comes upon us as we study, then the effort will have been worthwhile. Even though we have just touched on this matter, I hope that each reader will be moved by the profound and infinite mystery of it all.

Covering Apart from Sin

In a merely superficial reading of the Bible, God's protection seems to have to do only with sin, failure and our need to be clothed in the garments of salvation. But this is not the end of the matter. As we go deeper into the subject of covering, we realize that it has far greater significance than just protection from sin.

Before sin ever entered the world, there appears to have been a need for covering. We have already seen that Satan was once the anointed cherub whose purpose was to cover (see Ezekiel 28:14–16). The Hebrew word used in this passage for *guardian* means hedged in or enclosed. So this cherub evidently had a special responsibility as a protector or guardian.

So problematic are these two verses that most modern versions do not give an accurate translation. But it appears that Lucifer's job was covering, not from sin but in relation to the presence or glory of God. This took place before sin had ever entered the world.

In Isaiah 4:5 we read: "Over all the glory will be [or will be spread] a canopy." The Hebrew word that is used here for *canopy* is the word for covering or overlaying.

This takes us face-to-face with a mystery. The prophet was looking forward into eternity when there will be no more sin. Why then, when all that is evil has finally been destroyed, should there be a need for a covering "over all the glory"?

The New English Bible has a note saying that the Hebrew is obscure. But it is our understanding of the Hebrew that is obscure! *Over* is the same word that is used in the modern Hebrew language for the word *on*. So, on or over the glory there shall be a covering.

It seems that the covering will continue to be essential in the future, when there will be no sin and human failing, just as it was essential in the past before sin had entered the world. The need for covering will never end because it has to do with the glory of the Lord—which will continue forever.

The Glory of God

In Exodus 24:15–17 we read:

> When Moses went up on the mountain, the cloud covered it, and the glory of the LORD settled on Mount Sinai. For six days the cloud covered the mountain, and on the seventh day the LORD called to Moses from within the cloud. To the Israelites the glory of the LORD looked like a consuming fire on top of the mountain.

Moses asked to see God's glory, and God said:

> I will cause all my goodness to pass in front of you, and I will proclaim my name, the LORD, in your presence ... but ... you cannot see my face, for no one may see me and live.
> Exodus 33:19–20

Then the Lord said to Moses,

> There is a place near me where you may stand on a rock. When my glory passes by, I will put you in a cleft in the rock and cover you with my hand until I have passed by. Then I will

remove my hand and you will see my back; but my face must
not be seen.

Exodus 33:21–23

Why was it necessary for God to shield Moses, one of the most
righteous men who has ever lived? Why should he be hidden,
covered, when God showed Himself to him? One day every
one of us is going to see the glory of the Lord. But the glory of
the Lord could destroy us now unless we are covered.

Now consider Isaiah 4:5–6:

> Then the Lord will create over all of Mount Zion and over
> those who assemble there a cloud of smoke by day and a glow
> of flaming fire by night; over all the glory will be a canopy. It
> will be a shelter and shade from the heat of the day, and a
> refuge and hiding place from the storm and rain.

The Tabernacle

This connection between the glory of the Lord and a covering
can be seen again and again in the Old Testament.

For instance, when the Tabernacle was erected we read,
"Then the cloud covered the Tent of Meeting, and the glory of
the Lord filled the tabernacle" (Exodus 40:34). In Numbers
9:15–16 we read:

> On the day the tabernacle, the Tent of the Testimony, was set
> up, the cloud covered it. From evening till morning the cloud
> above the tabernacle looked like fire. That is how it continued
> to be; the cloud covered it, and at night it looked like fire.

The Tabernacle, which was filled with the glory of the Lord, is
one of the greatest symbols in the Old Testament. Every article
in this tent was richly symbolic of God's dwelling place on
earth, a pattern of heavenly things. In Hebrews 9 we are shown
the parallel between the Tabernacle and Christ's sacrifice.

Exodus 26 describes how the fabric of the tent was made of
finely twined linen, interwoven with figures of cherubim that
could only be seen from the inside. Curtains of plain black
goat hair were placed as a covering over the Tabernacle,
hanging over the sides to cover it completely. Over this there
were two further coverings, one of ram's skins that were dyed
red, and the other of sealskins.

These layers of physical coverings, along with the emblems of the cherubim, give a vivid picture of spiritual covering in relation to God's glory and absolute holiness.

The Cherubim and Seraphs

The cherubim are a composite symbol of God's glory and power as Creator. We find them also in Revelation 4:6–8 where they are described as surrounding the throne of God.

Whoever was recorded in Scripture as glimpsing the cherubim was always struck by their wings. Ezekiel 1:23 describes them as angelic beings with three pairs of wings. Only one pair is used for flying—two pairs are used for covering.

In three different places in the Bible, we read how the wings of the cherubim were to cover the Ark of the Covenant. One of these is found in 2 Chronicles 5:7–8:

> The priests then brought the ark of the LORD's covenant to its place in the inner sanctuary of the temple, the Most Holy Place, and put it beneath the wings of the cherubim. The cherubim spread their wings over the place of the ark and covered the ark and its carrying poles.

So in the holiest place of the Temple were two huge cherubim. Their wingspan together stretched from wall to wall, covering the mercy seat and the Ark of the Covenant, the outward symbol of the presence of God.

The glory of the Lord appeared there, and God communed with the high priest. That was where the covering provided by these huge wings was needed. The cherubim speak of the glory, grace and power of God.

In Isaiah's vision of the Lord (Isaiah 6:1–3), he was aware of seraphs, which are rather like cherubim:

> I saw the Lord seated on a throne, high and exalted, and the train of his robe filled the temple. Above him were seraphs, each with six wings: With two wings they covered their faces, with two they covered their feet, and with two they were flying. And they were calling to one another:
>
> > "Holy, holy, holy is the LORD Almighty;
> > the whole earth is full of his glory."

The wings are emblems of covering, again connected with God's glory.

The Majesty of God

The majesty of God, His infinite greatness and what the Puritans used to call "the unutterable holiness of God" are rarely appreciated today. You have to go a long way in Christian circles to hear someone preach on the majesty of God.

We have tended to make God small and cozy in our own conception. We have lowered Him to our own level of understanding, making Him more mundane, more ordinary. We think we can put God under a microscope and examine Him. In some theological colleges and seminaries, it is as if God has been taken apart by a categorization of His attributes, analyzed and then put back together again.

When we do this, whether at an academic level or in our home Bible study groups, we no longer have a sense of His infinity, greatness and awe. Instead, we are left with a God who is reduced to the size of our own finite minds.

But God is God, eternal and unchangeable. Some think that in the Old Testament He was all fire and in the New Testament He was all grace, as if He had somehow evolved or changed His mind. What nonsense! Each generation may emphasize different aspects of God's nature, but His essential character remains the same.

The same God who caused the Sinai to smoke like a furnace is the God we have come to know today through Jesus Christ. To this very day He is consuming power, infinite in power and majesty, unutterably holy.

The heaven of heavens cannot contain the living God. Even if there are billions and billions of universes, it will not exhaust Him or limit Him.

There is no end to God's power and greatness. So, no finite created being, let alone you or I, can ever fully comprehend Him. The twenty-first century has not made anything more difficult for Him. Yes, our "scientific" worldview in the West has limited our own capacity to experience Him, and where people have not put God in a "box," He more often works in power. But God is still God—regardless of what culture we are in!

How wonderful that God became a human being. Just as Jesus was fully God but fully man, so the infinite God can be known as *Abba, Father*. Yet we do not become familiar with Him in a disrespectful and irreverent way.

God is love, but He is also power and righteousness and holiness. If the glory of God were to be fully released upon us, it would be as if we had been shriveled up by the force of a million volts. In Christ alone can we approach the infinite power and holiness of God and yet remain absolutely safe.

One day we shall see God. Revelation 22:4 tells us that the servants of God "will see his face." Then we will be covered only by the righteousness of Christ.

We are touching a mystery. Covering has to do with the infinite power of God. If we truly saw and understood that for what it is, then the fear of the Lord, the beginning of wisdom (see Proverbs 1:7), would truly come upon us all.

Study questions:

1. How is covering portrayed in the Bible, apart from the existence of sin?
2. What does Moses' experience on the mountain tell us about covering?
3. What do the Tabernacle, seraphs and cherubim show us about covering and God's glory?
4. How have we lost the sense of God's majesty and infinite holiness in our modern culture?
5. How are you beginning to grasp something of the awesome mystery of God's covering?

Lance Lambert studied at the School of Oriental and African Studies (University of London) and currently lives in Jerusalem. He is the author of *Uniqueness of Israel, Till the Day Dawn, Spiritual Character, Watch and Pray, Battle for Israel, Spiritual Covering, Love Divine* and *Jacob I Have Loved.*